THE NBA FINALS

BY MATT LILLEY

Apex is distributed by North Star Editions:
sales@northstareditions.com | 888-417-0195

Produced for Apex by Red Line Editorial.

Photographs ©: Steven Senne/AP Images, cover, 8–9; Carlos Avila Gonzalez/San Francisco Chronicle/AP Images, 1, 4–5, 18–19; Michael Dwyer/AP Images, 6; Wikimedia, 10–11; Library of Congress, 13; iStockphoto, 14, 15, 29; Shutterstock Images, 16–17; Luis M. Alvarez/AP Images, 20–21; Lennox McLendon/AP Images, 22–23; Mike Blake/Reuters/Alamy, 24; Ron Schwane/AP Images, 27

Library of Congress Control Number: 2022912147

ISBN
978-1-63738-293-6 (hardcover)
978-1-63738-329-2 (paperback)
978-1-63738-399-5 (ebook pdf)
978-1-63738-365-0 (hosted ebook)

Printed in the United States of America
Mankato, MN
012023

NOTE TO PARENTS AND EDUCATORS
Apex books are designed to build literacy skills in striving readers. Exciting, high-interest content attracts and holds readers' attention. The text is carefully leveled to allow students to achieve success quickly. Additional features, such as bolded glossary words for difficult terms, help build comprehension.

TABLE OF CONTENTS

CHAPTER 1

THE 2022 FINALS

The Golden State Warriors have led for most of Game 6. They are facing the Boston Celtics in the National Basketball Association (NBA) Finals. Less than six minutes are left in the game.

Stephen Curry (30) scored 34 points for the Golden State Warriors in Game 6 of the 2022 NBA Finals.

The Celtics hit a three-pointer. Now they're down only eight points. But the Warriors also hit a three.

FAST FACT

In 2022, the Warriors reached their sixth Finals in eight years.

Jaylen Brown led the Boston Celtics in points during Game 6.

Curry holds the Finals MVP trophy and celebrates winning the 2022 Finals.

Then the Warriors force a turnover. Boston loses the ball to them. The Warriors score. They hold on to the lead. The clock runs out. The Warriors are NBA **champions**.

FINALS MVP

In 2022, Stephen Curry won his fourth Finals with Golden State. He was also named the Finals Most Valuable Player (MVP). That was a first for Curry.

CHAPTER 2

NBA HISTORY

People started playing basketball in the 1890s. The game quickly became popular. The first **professional league** formed in 1898.

James Naismith invented basketball in 1891.

In 1947, the first Finals took place. The Philadelphia Warriors beat the Chicago Stags.

FAST FACT

The Minneapolis Lakers joined pro basketball in 1948. They won five Finals in their first six years.

Bob Cousy (left) was an early NBA star. He played for Boston in the 1950s and early 1960s.

As of 2022, Charlotte, North Carolina, was the most recent city to get a new NBA team.

In the 1960s, the NBA was steadily adding teams. The league had 12 teams in 1967–68. By 2004–05, 30 teams were in the NBA. Then no new teams joined for a while.

WORLDWIDE

The NBA is based in the United States. But the league draws players from dozens of countries. It also has international fans. People from all around the world watch the NBA Finals.

In 2022, the Toronto Raptors were the only NBA team outside the United States. They won the Finals in 2019.

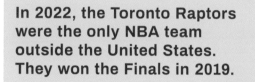

CHAPTER 3

THE PATH TO THE FINALS

Two **conferences** make up the NBA. One is the Eastern Conference. The other is the Western Conference. The best teams in each conference go to the **playoffs**.

Madison Square Garden has been home to the Eastern Conference's New York Knicks since 1968.

The playoffs have four rounds. Teams that win one round move on to the next. Teams that lose are knocked out.

BEST OF SEVEN

Each playoff round is a best of seven. Teams play each other up to seven times. The team that wins four games wins the round.

Ja Morant (left) and the Memphis Grizzlies lost in the second round of the 2022 playoffs.

The third round is the conference finals. Conference champions go to the NBA Finals. The Eastern champion plays the Western champion.

The Miami Heat won their first Finals in 2006.

FAST FACT

As of 2022, two teams had 17 **titles**. The Boston Celtics and the Los Angeles Lakers shared the **record**.

CHAPTER 4

FINALS HIGHLIGHTS

Two **legends** faced off in the 1984 NBA Finals. Magic Johnson's Lakers played Larry Bird's Celtics. The Celtics won. Bird was voted Finals MVP.

Magic Johnson (left) and Larry Bird played many exciting games against each other.

In 1998, the Utah Jazz nearly won Game 6. Then Michael Jordan stole the ball. He made a 20-foot shot. The Bulls won the game and the championship.

CHAMPION PLAYER

Bill Russell won more NBA championships than any other player. He played for 13 years. He won 11 championships with the Celtics.

Michael Jordan sinks a jumper to win Game 6 of the 1998 Finals.

The Cleveland Cavaliers were down three games to one in the 2016 Finals. Then LeBron James helped them win three straight games. The Cavs became champions.

FAST FACT

The Milwaukee Bucks won the Finals in 2021. It was their first championship in 50 years.

LeBron James won his third Finals MVP award for his amazing play in 2016.

COMPREHENSION QUESTIONS

Write your answers on a separate piece of paper.

1. Write a paragraph that explains the main ideas of Chapter 2.

2. Who is your favorite player in the NBA? Why?

3. Which team won the first NBA Finals?

    A. Chicago Stags

    B. Boston Celtics

    C. Philadelphia Warriors

4. Which team did Michael Jordan play for during the 1998 Finals?

    A. Utah Jazz

    B. Chicago Bulls

    C. Los Angeles Lakers

5. What does *turnover* mean in this book?

Then the Warriors force a turnover. Boston loses the ball to them. The Warriors score.

  A. time when the ball leaves the court
  B. loss of the ball to the other team
  C. end of a game

6. What does *international* mean in this book?

It also has international fans. People from all around the world watch the NBA Finals.

  A. from many states in the same country
  B. from just one country
  C. from many different countries

Answer key on page 32.

GLOSSARY

champions
Teams that win the final game in a conference or league.

conferences
Smaller groups of teams within a sports league.

league
A group of teams that play one another.

legends
People known for having great skill.

playoffs
A set of games played after the regular season to decide which team will be the champion.

professional
Having to do with people who get paid for what they do.

record
The best or fastest performance of all time.

titles
Top finishes in a sports competition.

TO LEARN MORE

BOOKS

Abdo, Kenny. *Miracle Moments in Basketball*. Minneapolis: Abdo Publishing, 2022.

Levit, Joe. *Meet Stephen Curry*. Minneapolis: Lerner Publications, 2023.

Morey, Allan. *The NBA Finals*. Minneapolis: Bellwether Media, 2019.

ONLINE RESOURCES

Visit **www.apexeditions.com** to find links and resources related to this title.

ABOUT THE AUTHOR

Matt Lilley has an MS in scientific and technical writing. The focus of his degree was on medical writing for kids. He loves researching and writing about all sorts of topics. He lives in Minnesota with his family.

INDEX

ANSWER KEY:
1. Answers will vary; 2. Answers will vary; 3. C; 4. B; 5. B; 6. C